Assignments 3

Assignments 3

The British Press Photographers'
Association Yearbook
Edited by Tom Hopkinson

Phaidon · Oxford

1 Brian Harris
George Bush waits in the wings to
'come on down' at a Republican Party
rally during the U.S. Presidential
Election campaign.
© *The Independent*

Phaidon Press Limited
Musterlin House
Jordan Hill Road
Oxford OX2 8DP

First published 1989

© The British Press Photographers'
Association 1989

A CIP catalogue record for this book is
available from the British Library.

ISBN 0 7148 2634 0

Designed by Alex Evans

Typeset in Gill Sans by
The Creative Text Partnership

Printed in Great Britain by
Butler & Tanner Limited, Frome

Contents

Introduction

by Tom Hopkinson

The photographs in this book cover a period from April 1988 to June 1989. Taken by members of the British Press Photographers' Association, they present what may appear to be mainly a record of disaster and mishap, over a great part of the world.

Some of these tragic events can be described as 'accidents'; some were the consequence of men working for long periods under pressure in dangerous situations; some – notably the Chinese massacre – were the result of conflicts, social and political, which could, and should, have been resolved by peaceful means.

The world, it must seem to many, is becoming an increasingly dangerous place. Over vast areas of Africa famines have raged unchecked. In East Asia hordes of people have been expelled from their homes, often setting out on desperate voyages to escape unbearable conditions. In Latin America and elsewhere, natural resources, accumulated over millions of years, are being recklessly squandered for immediate profit. The very atmosphere surrounding us is contaminated, and the earth's protective covering is being dissipated with consequences no one can foresee.

Disasters, however, are only one side of the contemporary scene, and the fact that, for the first time in history, we are able to see so much of what is happening all over our planet is a different – and reassuring – aspect.

No more than fifty years ago, when British and French governments turned a blind eye to Hitler's invasion of Czechoslovakia, a British prime minister, Neville Chamberlain, could speak of Czechoslovakia as 'a far-off country of which people in this country know little'. And therefore, it was implied, we need not concern ourselves about its fate. Against such an attitude we can set the efforts which individuals and organizations make today to help people they will never know, in parts of the world they will never see.

That protective layer of callousness, which has allowed one part of mankind to remain blind to what is happening to the rest, is being rapidly stripped away. And this is happening not mainly out of high principles, but as the result of technical progress. Developments in radio and telephonic communication and in satellite observation have made it possible – and in the long run essential – for the world to become one place, and to recognize itself as such.

Acceptance of English as the world's second language, taking place without offical decision and almost, as it were, unnoticed, has provided an essential link between nations, as has also the spectacular growth in industry, commerce, and the network of air communication.

A few politicians still struggle to maintain

Introduction

separate control over national states – just as in Africa some leaders continue to think and act along tribal lines – but for finance, industry and commerce, national boundaries have already become almost meaningless.

And now, within the brief period covered by this book, two developments have occurred, quite beyond expectation, which seem set to erase national frontiers yet further, draw humanity closer together, and project a new image of man's position in the world.

The progressive demolition of the barriers between East and West, initiated by the Soviet leader Mikhail Gorbachev, marks – it may be hoped – the beginning of the end of the artificial separation of mankind into two hostile camps. A spirit of co-operation may, in the next decade, free both sides from the huge burden of costly weaponry maintained 'to preserve peace', and enable living standards to be improved, particularly in the Eastern bloc. Such co-operation may also lead to a much wider association in science, art, industry and commerce, which can make the immense achievements of the past hundred years seem slender by comparison.

Russell Schweickhart, an American astronaut in the Apollo flight of 1969, wrote in his book *The Home Planet:* 'I believe that space is the future of the world, that there will be a movement of humanity away from the earth. In the centuries to come there will be more people living off the earth than on it.'

And now, with the arrival on the political scene of Green parties and Green policies, there opens out for humanity a new and far more satisfying role in the universe. For centuries there has existed – in the minds of poets, philosophers and religious leaders – the idea of the world as a garden or estate, with mankind as its keeper and protector. In the past this existed only as a dream. But already it seems likely that men and women of tomorrow will regard themselves as responsible for the planet as a whole; for the creatures with whom they share it; and for the natural resources they inherited.

They will see themselves as protectors, not merely as consumers; as guardians rather than exploiters, responsible for passing on to the future a world as good as – or better than – the one they have inhabited.

This year marks the 150th anniversary of the invention of photography. A harmless pastime for the well-to-do, it appeared at the time to have little practical significance. But today that pastime has become the chief source of information and the most important means of communication across the globe. The size of television audiences, and the amount of time spent watching programmes of news and current affairs, attest to its pre-eminence.

Newspapers too are increasingly aware of the power of the still picture. The myth

2 Jon Jones
Nigel Lawson prepares for his budget-day photocall.
March 1989.
© *The Independent*

8

that print depends on words – with pictures in a secondary role, employed, as old-timers would say, 'to lighten the page' – persisted for long but is at last beginning to change.

Following the example of *The Independent,* daily and Sunday newspapers are giving greater space to photographs and a higher status to cameramen. Press photographers, with their colleagues in television, have become the eyes of the world. How well they understand, and how courageously and skilfully they carry out their

arduous task, the following pages amply demonstrate.

Verbal reporting of the Chinese conflict, both by newspaper and television journalists, has been notably good. But the photograph in this book showing the line of soldiers grimly advancing across Tiananmen Square, while the students in the foreground recognize for the first time what they are up against, tells more than any words.

Almost thirty years ago I was in the Congo as a reporter, working with and

Introduction

alongside a group of cameramen. I noted of them at the time: 'A bunch of true professionals; quick-witted as weasels; hard-boiled as jockeys; wary, astute, hard-working. Always alert to steal a march, they were equally ready to share a chance, give a lift, or cover up for one who had missed the boat.'

'Their company did me good. I wished I had a newspaper or magazine that could hire the lot.'

Being the eyes of the world, however, is no easy task. Of the four who were my companions, at a time when not only the Congo but much of Africa appeared to be going up in smoke, one, Larry Burrows, died some ten years later when his helicopter was shot down in Vietnam. Another, TV cameraman Ernie Christie, flew his light plane head on into the side of an apartment block. The third, Barry von Below, survived to become the much-esteemed picture editor of the *Johannesburg Star*, until his death some years ago. Only one of the four, Ian Berry, still follows his exacting calling.

News photographers, by my scale of values, are a much underrated body – underrated at times even by their editors and writing colleagues. They deserve a lot more recognition and appreciation than they get; and if this book helps them to secure it, the efforts of all those responsible will have been well worth while.

Tom Hopkinson

3 John Downing
The missiles are going: Russians depart from East Germany with their SS12 ballistic missiles after the Reagan-Gorbachev summit.
February 1989
© *Daily Express*

4 Herbie Knott
Army manœuvres: Soldier in the snow during NATO exercises in West Germany.
November 1988
© Herbie Knott

5 Herbie Knott
Kurdish refugee, Turkey. December 1988
© Herbie Knott

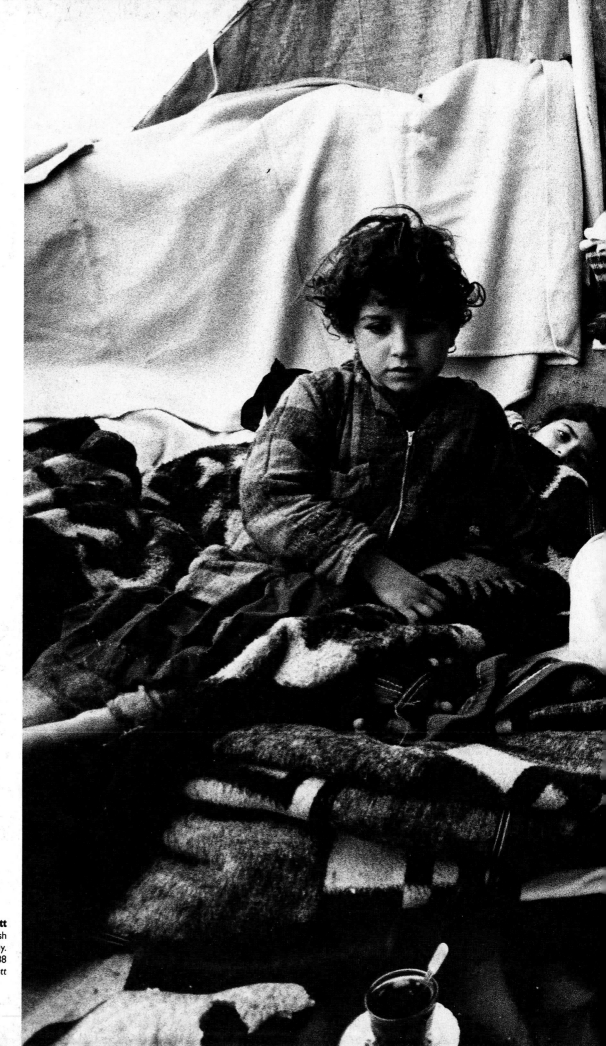

6 Herbie Knott
Homeless: Kurdish
refugees, Turkey.
December 1988
© *Herbie Knott*

7 Bob Gannon
The Salman Rushdie
protest: Muslim
demonstration against
The Satanic Verses,
Central London.
January 1989
© *Bob Gannon*

8 John Chapman
Yasser Arafat addresses the United Nations General Assembly, Geneva.
December 1988
© *John Chapman*

9 Frank Martin
Ayatollah passes on: Hysteria victim at the funeral of Ayatollah Khomeini, Iran.
June 1989
© *The Guardian*

10 Michael Steele
Track cycling,
Leicester.
© *The Independent*

11 John Downing
The *Virgin Challenger* breaks the transatlantic speed record.
© *Daily Express*

12 Tim Bishop
Nigel Lawson receives a stern rebuke at the Conservative
Women's Conference. March 1989
© *The Times*

13 John Chapman
Michael Heseltine campaigning for Dudley Fishburn (left)
in the Kensington by-election. July 1989
© *John Chapman*

14 Tim Bishop
Health minister Kenneth Clarke at the Conservative
Women's Conference. March 1989
© *The Times*

15 David Sillitoe
Setting a good example: Thatcher litter photocall in St James's Park, London.
© *The Guardian*

16 Sean Smith
Going or coming? SDP Leader David
Owen.
© *The Guardian*

17 Tim Bishop
Dennis Healey dances with Kensington by-election
candidate Ann Holmes at an OAP centre in Notting
Hill Gate. July 1988
© The Times

18 Brian Harris
Democratic presidential candidate Michael Dukakis
'pumping the flesh' on his victory train ride through
California. October 1988
© The Independent

19 Julian Herbert
The nose section of the
Pan Am jumbo jet which
was destroyed by a
terrorist bomb over
Lockerbie in Scotland.
December 1988
© *The Times*

20 David Rose
The hills above Lockerbie.
Flags mark the positions of
the bodies. December 1988
© *The Independent*

21 David Rose
Lockerbie disaster: The
morning after. December
1988
© *The Independent*

22 David Rose
The night's catastrophe awaits one
Lockerbie resident. December 1988
© *The Independent*

23 Mark Pepper
Back from the yacht: Revellers come ashore during Cowes Week
celebrations at the Royal Yacht Squadron, Isle of Wight. July 1988
© The Times

25 Sue Adler
Enthusiasts: Members of the Victorian Society at the Brompton Cemetery by the
grave of Val Prinsep, painter. May 1989
© Sue Adler

26 David Rose
Good Friday Republican memorial service: masked man gives an IRA address with
Gerry Adams, president of Sinn Fein, in the background looking on. April 1989
© The Independent

27 Crispin Rodwell
Class-mates of 13-year-old Emma Donnelly at her graveside in Benburb, County
Tyrone. She was killed with her grandfather in an IRA bombing. November 1988
© Crispin Rodwell

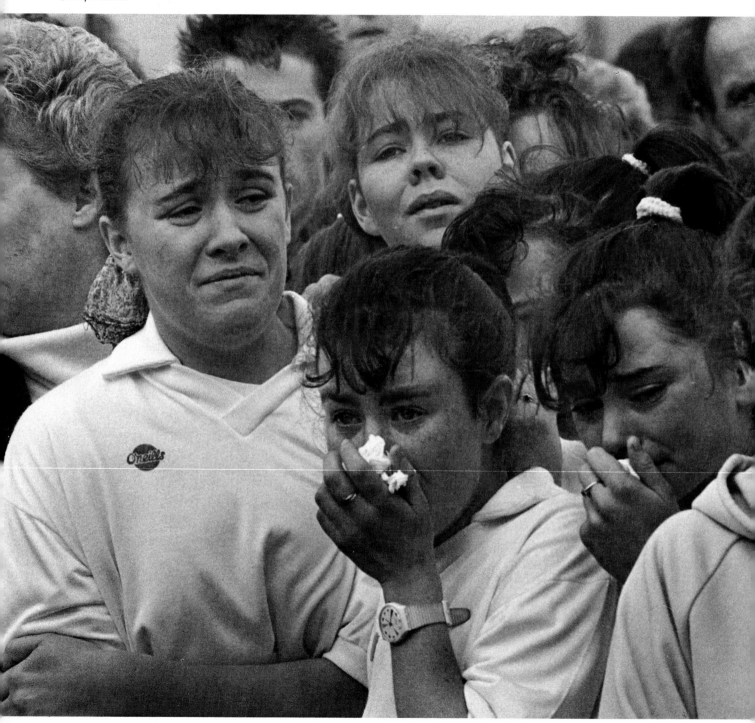

28 Crispin Rodwell
A fatal blast: Seconds after an IRA bomb ripped naval officer Alan Shields' car apart in Belfast. He was killed instantly by the booby trap as he made his way home.
August 1988
© Crispin Rodwell

29 Crispin Rodwell
Soldiers wait to go into West Belfast to quell rioting which broke out after the extradition of IRA man Robert Russell. The ambulance was carrying a soldier injured by a bomb explosion.
© Crispin Rodwell

30 Mark Pepper
Mime artist: Marcel Marceau in his London hotel room. July 1988
© *The Times*

31 Jon Jones
Composer: Olivier Messiaen with his wife in London.
© *The Independent*

33 Herbie Knott
Ballet Class: The Kirov Ballet rehearsals attract a young audience in London. July 1988
© *Herbie Knott*

Actor: Mickey Rooney goes on stage in London.
© *Daily Express*

35 Simon Townsley
Director: Jonathan Miller, Old Vic
theatre artistic director.
© *The Sunday Times*

36 Michael Ward
Anything you can do...: *Hobson's Choice*, a new ballet choreographed by David
Bintley to the music of Paul Reade. Michael O'Hare, of the Sadlers Wells Royal
Ballet, dances the character of Will Mossop at the Royal Opera House, Covent
Garden. February 1989
© *Sunday Times*

37 Simon Grosset
...I can do better: Jane Finnie, winner of the Genée Award for
classical dancing (and £1,500). January 1989
© *The Daily Telegraph*

Over page:
38 Herbie Knott
The Clapham rail disaster. December 1988
© *Herbie Knott*

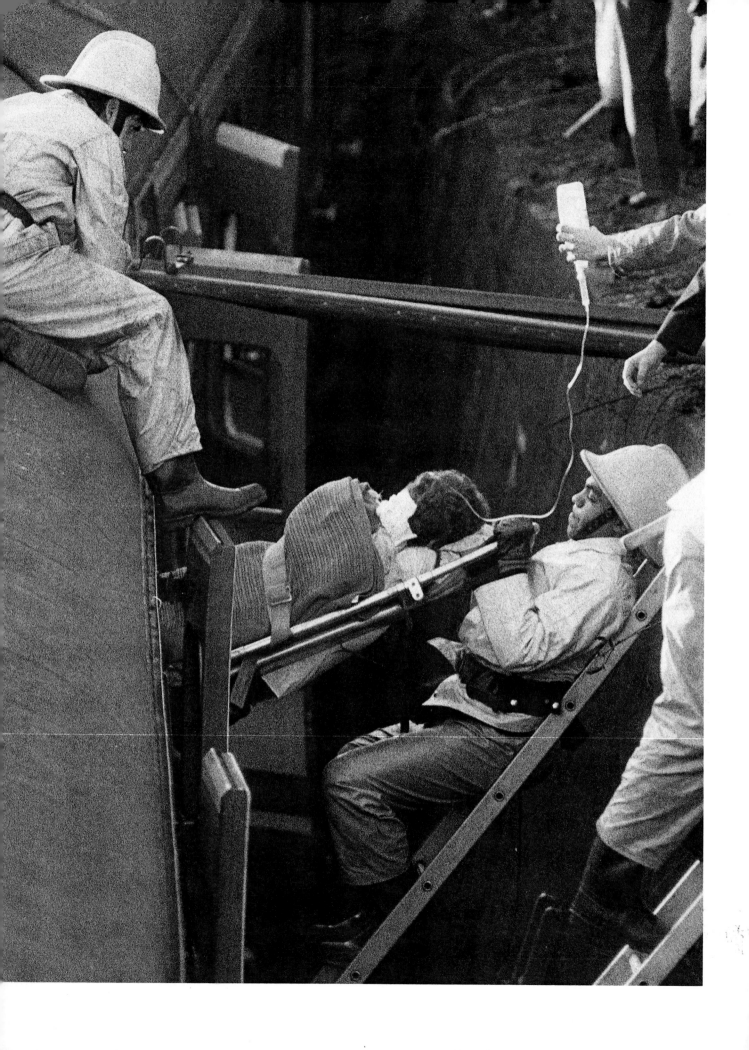

39 David Rose
A difficult rescue
following the Clapham
rail disaster.
December 1988
© *The Independent*

40 Steve Poole
Rail crash at Staples
Corner, Hendon.
March 1989
© *Daily Mail*

41 Sean Smith
Rail crash at Purley: Removing the debris. March 1989
© *The Guardian*

43 Roger Bamber
Churdling the Spurdle: Retired Squadron Leader Alf Lords in traditional milking
smock for a game of churdle the spurdle in Chardstock, Devon. Prize for the
fastest churdler is a live pig. October 1988
© Roger Bamber

44 Graham Turner
Pig racing in Ireland.
© *The Guardian*

45 Simon Grossett
Husky racing in Radnor Forest on the Welsh border. March 1989
© *The Daily Telegraph*

46 Brian Harris
Not interested in sport: Organic farming.
© *The Independent*

47 Nick Rogers
Lone master rejoins battle with the sea. It is twenty years since Robin Knox-
Johnston returned to a hero's welcome at Falmouth in his sturdy, 32-foot ketch,
Suhaili, to become the first man to sail round the world alone and non-stop. He
renewed his lonely partnership at Plymouth for the Carlsberg single-handed
transatlantic race. June 1988
© *The Times*

48   Denzil McNeelance
Journey's end. Big Ben shows exactly 4.30, and for Terry Glanville, aged 67, a hard seven hours is thankfully over as he completes the London Marathon. April 1988
© *The Times*

49 Steve Poole
Wimbledon 1988: Martina
Navratilova celebrates
her win over Helena
Sukova. June 1988
© *Daily Mail*

50 Marc Aspland
Boat race on the
River Thames.
© *The Times*

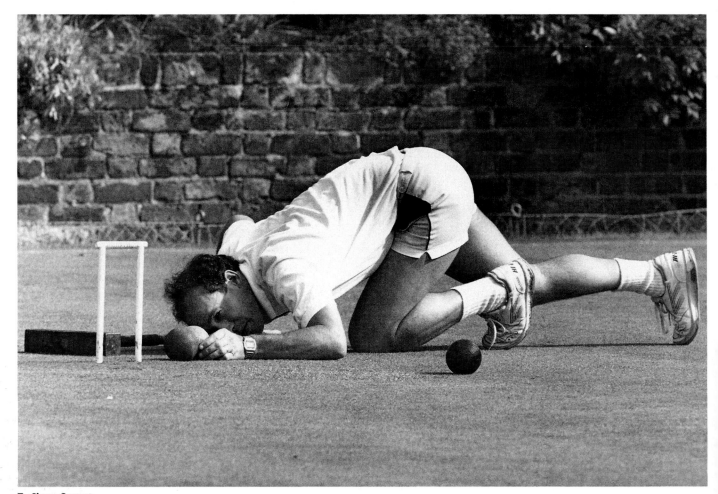

Я Simon Grosset
Stephen Mulliner, croquet champion, at the World Croquet Championships,
London. September 1988
© *Daily Telegraph*

52 Tim Bishop
Wimbledon 1988: Kevin Curren suffers an ankle injury in the second round, which
forces him to retire from the championships. June 1988
© The Times

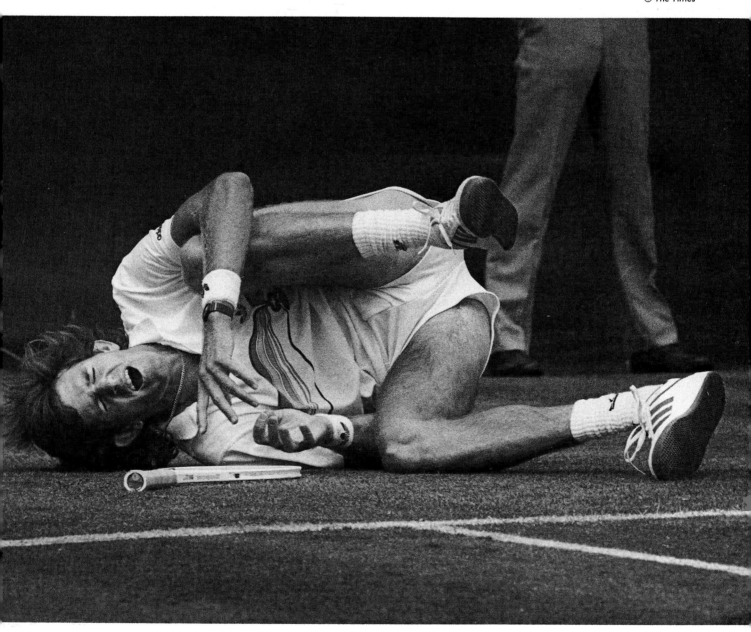

53 Howard Walker
Liverpool's Ray Houghton shoots for the goal.
© *Sunday Mirror*

54 Howard Walker
The Hillsborough disaster: Fans trapped against the perimeter fencing. April 1989
© *Sunday Mirror*

Over page:
55 Howard Walker
The Hillsborough disaster:
Liverpool fans escape the crush. April 1989
© *Sunday Mirror*

56 Howard Walker
The Hillsborough disaster: Police and fans use advertising
hoardings as makeshift stretchers. April 1989
© *Sunday Mirror*

58 Howard Walker
The Hillsborough disaster: Police and fans
attend to the injured. April 1989
© *Sunday Mirror*

57 Howard Walker
The Hillsborough disaster: A Liverpool fan
gives the kiss of life. April 1989
© *Sunday Mirror*

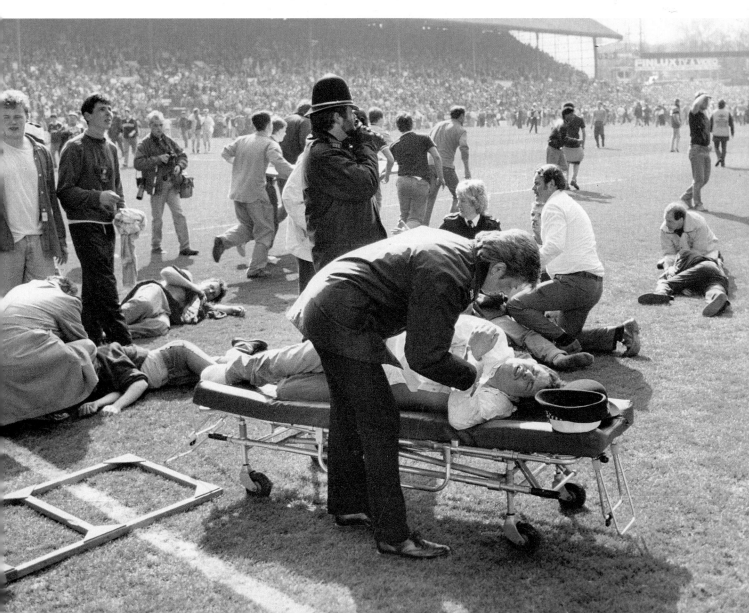

59 Howard Walker
The Hillsborough disaster: Shocked survivors
comfort each other. April 1989
© *Sunday Mirror*

60   Howard Walker
The aftermath of the Hillsborough disaster: A fan mourns the victims on the kop
at Liverpool. April 1989
© *Sunday Mirror*

61 Tom Stoddart
Desert Folly: President Houphouet-
Boigny of the Ivory Coast is building a
basilica only one foot smaller than St
Peter's in Rome. The cathedral is
being built at Younoussoukro, the
President's home village. Meanwhile
his subjects scavenge for food and
firewood on the edge of the giant
building site.
© *Tom Stoddart*

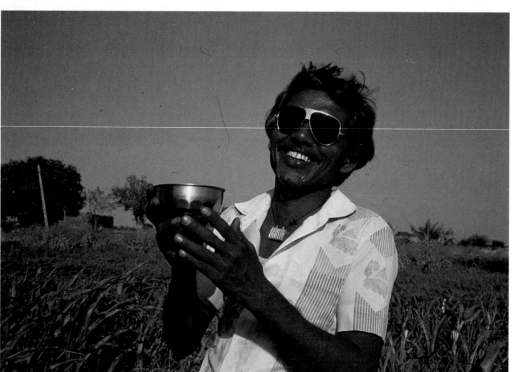

62 Tom Stoddart
Ishwar Valji Parmar, who is blind after drinking illicit hooch in Gandhi's home state of Gujarat, India. Hundreds of people died after drinking the lattha. Ishmar used to be a night-watchman. He is holding his baby son, Roshan.
© Tom Stoddart

63 Tom Stoddart
The mafia middleman who sells the illicit drink to the poor of Gujarat. He buys the hooch from stills in the countryside.
© Tom Stoddart

64 Stuart Nicol
The British Midland Airways jet which failed to reach the runway at East Midlands airport, falling six hundred feet short and crashing on the embankment of the M1 motorway.
January 1989
© Stuart Nicol

65 Stuart Nicol
Women and children stand by what remains of their home following the floods that
hit Khartoum, Sudan, after the River Nile burst its banks. August 1988
© Stuart Nicol

66 Stuart Nicol
Floods in Sudan.
© *Stuart Nicol*

67 Stuart Nicol
Piper Alpha: The fiery remains of the North Sea oil rig. July 1988
© Stuart Nicol

68 Howard Walker
A sad Princess of Wales visiting the injured of the Piper Alpha explosion.
July 1988
© *Sunday Mirror*

69 Stuart Nicol
A gold miner at Cotia
gold mine, North Brazil.
The miners are called
'garimpo', meaning 'ant
worker'. October 1988
© *Stuart Nicol*

70 Dario Mitidieri
Student rally in Tiananmen Square, Beijing. June 1989
© *Dario Mitidieri*

71 Bob Gannon
Student march through Beijing. May 1989
© Bob Gannon

72 Dario Mitidieri
Writing for illegal leaflets in Tiananmen Square.
June 1989
© Dario Mitidieri

73   Dario Mitidieri
People applaud the pro-democracy statue in
Tiananmen Square. June 1989
© Dario Mitidieri

74   Bob Gannon
Students receive donated food at dusk,
Tiananmen Square. May 1989
© Bob Gannon

75 Dario Mitidieri
Night-time in Tiananmen Square.
June 1989
© *Dario Mitidieri*

76 Dario Mitidieri
Early morning in Tiananmen Square.
June 1989
© *Dario Mitidieri*

77 Bob Gannon
An injured soldier is helped away from Tiananmen Square by students after the
military launched an unsuccessful attempt to rush the square unarmed and on foot.
June 1989
© Bob Gannon

78 Dario Mitidieri
Democratic protesters watch as the army occupies Tiananmen Square, which had been
the focal point of the student-led peaceful demonstration for democracy. June 1989
© Dario Mitidieri

79 Dario Mitidieri
A civilian hurries away from Tiananmen Square after its occupation by the army during the night of 3-4 June. Army vehicles can be seen still burning after the clashes with the democratic protesters. June 1989
© Dario Mitidieri

80 Dario Mitidieri
Democratic protesters drag a wrecked truck to form a barricade against the
occupying army forces, Tiananmen Square. June 1989
© Dario Mitidieri

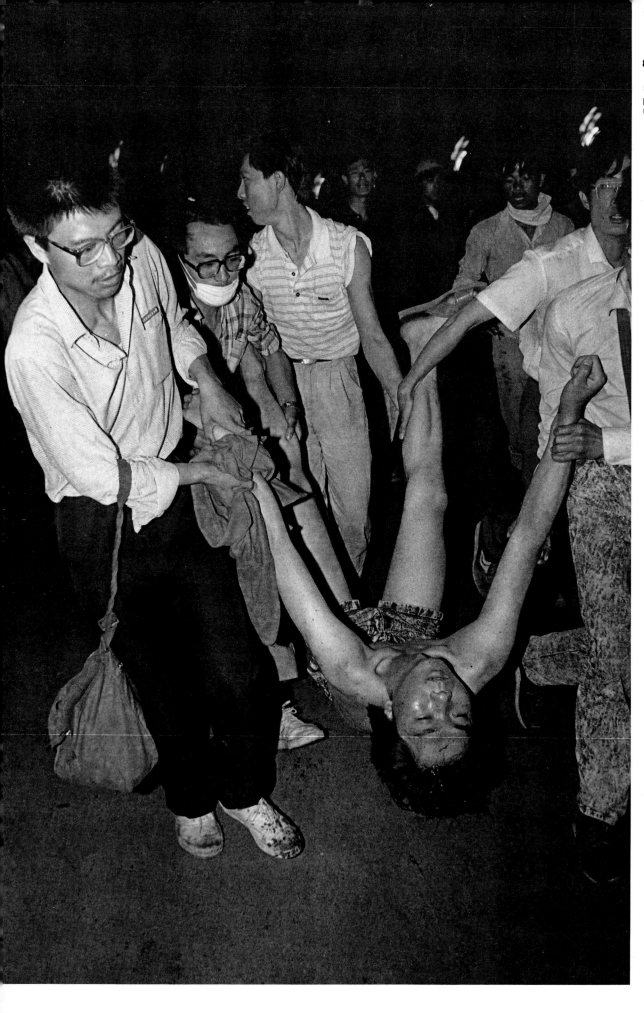

81 Dario Mitidieri
A student shot by the
army is carried away by
protestors. June 1989
© *Dario Mitidieri*

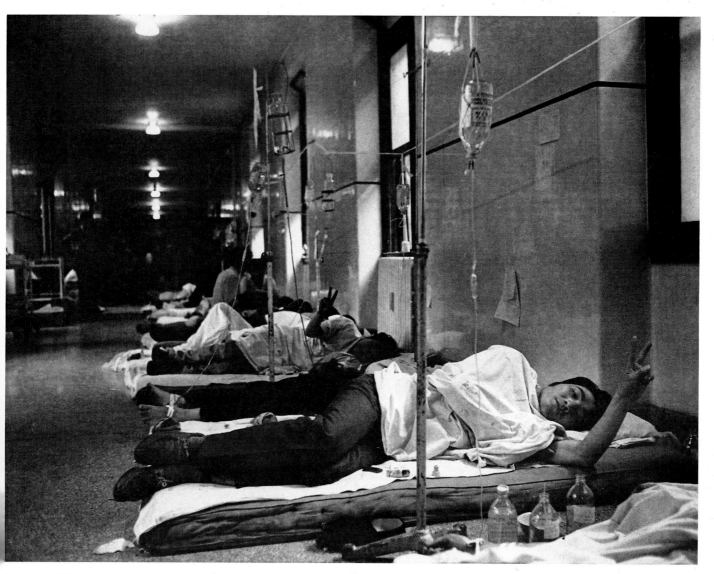

82 Dario Mitidieri
  Democratic protesters lie in a hospital ward after being wounded during the army
occupation of Tiananmen Square. June 1989
© *Dario Mitidieri*

83 Dario Mitidieri
Bodies of protesters piled up in the corner of a hospital after the army occupation
of Tiananmen Square. June 1989
© *Dario Mitidieri*

Assignment:
China and Iran

When Dario Mitidieri was planning to cover the student protests in Beijing, he was advised that there was little point in going: the story was considered to be over. It was nearing the end of May and the students' non-violent uprising against the Chinese government had already been going on for five weeks.

When Mitidieri arrived, with fellow photographer Bob Gannon, there was indeed a lull – yet nine days later the government sent in troops and tanks against the unarmed protesters of Tiananmen Square in a brutal crackdown. Mitidieri and Gannon were the only British press photographers there and for both it was an overwhelming experience.

'It was probably the first time in which I really felt that I was accomplishing the purpose of my work,' says Mitidieri. 'I felt for the first time that I was there to record something. Normally, in this job, you're doing very ordinary stories, but you never really feel that the world relies on you, as the press. China wouldn't have let the world know what was going on if we hadn't been there.'

Reports of the massacre eclipsed news of another major event at the same weekend: the death of Ayatollah Khomeini ten years after founding Iran's Islamic Republic. Such was the fanatical frenzy at his burial, the following week, that it took many hours

before the Imam was finally laid to rest. To photograph the event, Frank Martin of *The Guardian* was sent to Teheran at short notice, having spent the Sunday morning covering a dance festival in Paddington.

As with Tiananmen Square, the assignment required more than technical skill. As well as needing to adapt quickly to an alien environment, all three photographers had to work in extreme circumstances on very little sleep.

'A large part of the job is logistics,' says Martin. 'You just have to use your initiative. The actual photography is only a small part and it has to be pretty automatic.'

Iranian officials had provided helicopters to transport the press to the graveside and there were too few for the many who wanted to board them. Nor were there enough soldiers at the grave to keep back the surging crowd. People died in the crush and Martin fell, injuring himself.

'The coverage was pretty horrendous,' he says, 'as they were all going berserk, beating their heads and chests. I didn't expect it to be so frantic, but out of chaos very often come good pictures.'

The mourners responded to Martin's presence with no more than curiosity, and when he fell they even came to his aid: one used his black headband to bandage Martin's injured leg. Being the only British staff photographer there, Martin then had to

Assignment: China and Iran

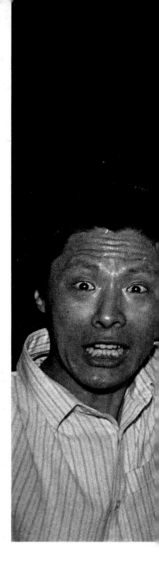

compete with the news agencies to wire his photographs back to London, after processing the film in a hotel bedroom. 'It would make a photographic tourist go white,' he remarks.

For some photographers, the very challenge of such assignments is often enough to carry them through the peril. 'You get a buzz being in the front line of something that is historic,' explains Martin.

Yet Gannon and Mitidieri had no desire to remain in Beijing after the carnage of 3 and 4 June. 'The history of photojournalism is steeped in horrific images,' says Bob Gannon. 'It's important to see certain things and witness certain events, but I don't thrive on adrenalin. There's a rush at first, but that happens in any violent situation. There's no courage involved – the real heroes are the subjects.'

In '88, after covering the IRA funerals at Milltown Cemetery through the grenade attack and the murder of the two British soldiers in Falls Road, Mitidieri had had nightmares for two weeks. The experience, however, enabled him to cope, to some degree, with the havoc of Tiananmen Square.

'You don't feel upset,' he says. 'You feel upset after, because everything is happening in front of you so quickly. This is nothing new, but people say that if you're behind a camera, you feel protected by it in a way. I think it's true to a certain extent. You feel less

vulnerable if you're looking at things through a little square.'

Neither he nor Gannon had expected violence.

Since the students had first expressed their discontent in April, while mourning the death of Hu Yaobang, the deposed liberal, there had been nationwide demonstrations. Gorbachev's historic visit had been upstaged and the humiliated authorities had imposed martial law.

When Gannon and Mitidieri arrived, the students were discussing ending their occupation of Tiananmen Square. Using a hotel room as base, Gannon and Mitidieri spent all their time with the students. The heat made it difficult to work during the day and they would stay up all night. Despite the relaxed and festive atmosphere, Gannon was aware of being watched by security police. Anonymous Chinese would emerge from the crowd, take his picture and disappear.

When the soldiers moved in, he and Mitidieri were having dinner at the Beijing Hotel. They rushed into the street without paying the bill and that was the last they saw of each other for the night. Nor did they know the fate of a female Chinese student, who had, till then, acted as their guide.

'When the situation broke, everyone was on their own,' says Mitidieri. 'In fact that was probably the most frightening thing – not even seeing other press around you.'

84 Dario Mitidieri
Wounded soldier rescued by students after his tank was destroyed. June 1989
© Dario Mitidieri

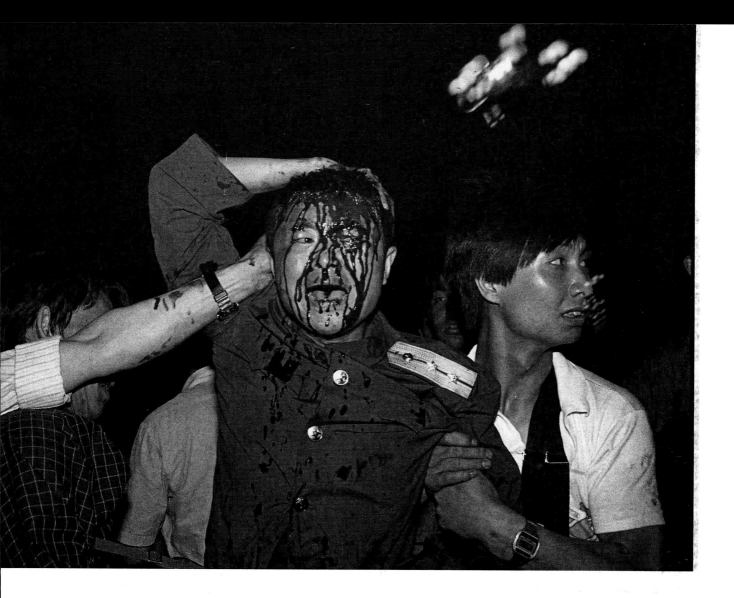

The first violent episode Mitidieri witnessed is recorded in a memorable photograph: a tank driver, with blood pouring down his head, being rescued by two students. The driver's vehicle was on fire and protesters had been beating him with metal chains.

After photographing other bloody incidents, Mitidieri left Tiananmen Square in the early morning, fearing that he would be trapped. The army was entering from three different directions and it was difficult to know from which point the shooting was coming. Hearing that the Beijing Hotel had been raided and that photographers were being searched, Mitidieri hid the film in his underpants and socks and found safety at another hotel.

Bob Gannon was less fortunate.

'I drifted off with this Dutch journalist,' he recalls. 'We got to a barricade of buses and suddenly people started screaming and running everywhere. I didn't know what was happening. Coming up the road was a

contingent of 70 or 80 soldiers, hidden behind these riot shields, looking really ominous in the street light, because it was pitch black. People instantly started throwing rocks and there was a full-scale riot.

Massive charges ensued. Gannon was at the front, rushing forward to take pictures and dodging the rocks. His eyes were streaming from the tear-gas attack, but he was able to carry on working, thanks to people providing damp cloths and pouring water on his head. For Gannon, one of the most shocking moments was the killing of a young soldier who had been cornered.

'They were dropping rocks into the centre of his face. I instantly tried to stop people doing it, which was a really automatic reaction. This was like a completely different scenario because in all the other things I'd watched, the students had helped the soldiers away.

'This was right in the middle of the street and I was completely mesmerized. I'll never forget watching this guy drop a rock on his

85 Dario Mitidieri
Student in her dormitory at
Peking University.
© Dario Mitidieri

face and just look up smiling. When I
staggered away, they were doing exactly the
same to another guy behind, who was
crawling through the grass.

Some tried to prevent Gannon from
taking pictures, but he doubts if they were
students. In the darkness, he had to use flash,
which drew unwanted attention to his
activities: each time he took a photograph,
everyone looked at him. It led to a highly
unpleasant encounter.

When he left the square and found refuge
in a hotel, he was attacked by five or six
security police. Gannon had just
photographed a row of dead and wounded
soldiers lying in the lobby.

'They got me up against the wall and
wrapped the camera strap round my neck. I
couldn't breathe. I was trying to give them
my equipment, saying "Take it! Take it!" and
they were slapping me across the face,
screaming at me in Chinese.'

Gannon's assailants removed the film
from his camera and took eight rolls of
valuable photographs from his pocket. He
was rescued by two American journalists,
who took him up to their rooms and locked
the door. 'I burst into tears and hid in the
shower. The situation had got so chaotic and
anarchic that I really thought they were going
to come up and get the Western journalists –
for defying martial law for one thing.'

On returning to England, Gannon felt
somewhat alienated. Within a short time,
events in China were no longer major news,
yet they remained vivid to him. 'I find that
bizarre,' he says, 'because it suddenly shows
you how fickle the whole thing is and how
distant news is diluted in a way.'

For Dario Mitidieri, the full horror of the
massacre struck him most forcibly when he
visited a hospital. By then, on the morning of
the 4th, Tiananmen Square was occupied by
the army. Tanks were patrolling the streets,
firing without provocation. Mitidieri set out
with one camera hidden beneath his jacket.
At the hospital, there were hundreds lying in
the corridors and people searching for
relatives. Mitidieri was shown a small room
containing a heap of corpses.

'Then I was really, really shocked,' he
says. 'I really just collapsed.'

Looking back on the experience, Bob
Gannon believes that it has matured him as a
photographer, while Dario Mitidieri now
views his previous work very differently.

'The stories I've been doing don't mean
anything to me any more. This is a story about
people who've been killed and were ready to
die for democracy. I witnessed that. I was part
of it to a certain extent and I photographed
it. Everything else which I've done is pretty
irrelevant.'

Josephine Glanville

86 Allan Titmuss
Alan Weekes, and
Cleveland Watkiss,
guitarist and vocalist
with The Jazz
Warriors, during a
rehearsal for an Arts
Council Contemporary
Music Network tour.
Queen Elizabeth Hall,
London. October 1988
© *Allan Titmuss*

87 Allan Titmuss
Whitney Houston at the National Exhibition Centre, Birmingham. May 1988
© *Allan Titmuss*

88 Allan Titmuss
Mark Knopfler and Eric Clapton. A warm-up concert for the Wembley Stadium
'Free Nelson Mandela' show. Hammersmith Odeon, London. June 1988
© *Allan Titmuss*

89 Allan Titmuss
Anita Baker at Wembley Arena, London. October 1988
© *Allan Titmuss*

90 Allan Titmuss
Anthony Braxton. The American composer and musician checks his mikes. Royalty Theatre, London. March 1989
© *Allan Titmuss*

91 Allan Titmuss
John Lee Hooker. Hammersmith Odeon, London. July 1988
© Allan Titmuss

92 Allan Titmuss
Julia Fordham. Dominion Theatre, London. November 1988
© Allan Titmuss

93 Allan Titmuss
Sonny Rollins. In the dressing-room painkillers and ice-packs did what they could to soothe a painful tooth, but on stage he was his usual self. Theatre Royal, Drury Lane, London. April 1989
© Allan Titmuss

94 Allan Titmuss
The Jazz Warriors. Some of the band wait to start a rehearsal. Queen Elizabeth Hall, London. October 1988
© Allan Titmuss

95 Chris Harris
Street scene. Camden Lock, London
© *The Times*

96 Michael Steele
Beach race,
Weston-super-Mare.
© The Independent

97 Chris Harris
Kate Stirling, hat-maker. London.
© *The Times*

98 Nick Rogers
Jean Muir, the guru of British Fashion. Dress sense: 'There's a compulsion to move all the time – move on shape, on proportion and colour – you can't help it,' Muir explains.
© *The Times*

99   John Downing
Sleeping rough.
© Daily Express

100 John Downing
Mafia killing in Palermo, Sicily.
© *Daily Express*

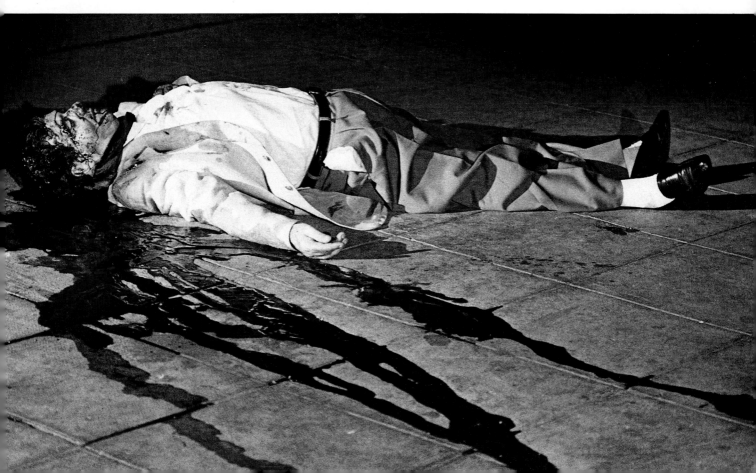

101 Mark Pepper
Still flying: Cecil
Lewis, aged 91, flying a
Tiger Moth over
Badminton,
Gloucestershire.
April 1989
© *The Times*

102   Bill Cross
Hatice Anutkam, the Turkish woman who, in desperation to hold her home and
children together after her husband left, sold one of her kidneys to the Humana
Hospital in London, creating a furore over the ethics of 'spare parts' private
surgery. February 1989
© Daily Mail

103 Alan Weller
Church leaders united: Britain's religious leaders entertained by a
squirrel at Lambeth Palace.
© *The Times*

104 Bryn Colton
Sick seal: A six-month-old grey seal, found with seal distemper off the Norfolk
coast, about to be taken to the seal rescue service centre.
© Bryn Colton

105 Tim Bishop
Saving the species: Glyn Griffiths, of the Welsh Hawking Centre, artificially
inseminates a peregrine falcon imprinted to believe that he is her mate. March 1989
© *The Times*

106 Mike Hollist
Friends: Dorsey, an injured fox, making friends with
chickens at an animal rescue centre in
Bournemouth.
© *Daily Mail*

107 Mark Pepper
Baby gorilla and mother.
© *The Times*

108 Mike Hollist
The old man: The gorilla compound at John Aspinall's zoo in Kent.
© *Daily Mail*

109 Mike Hollist
Orphans: Two young seals comfort each other after being rescued from the North Sea by Brenda Giles at King's Lynn, Norfolk.
© *Daily Mail*

110 Marc Aspland
Young rhinoceros
running with his keeper
at London Zoo.
© *The Times*

III   Chris Harris
Camden Lock, London.
© *The Times*

112 Bob Gannon
On the road to
Stonehenge. May 1988
© Bob Gannon

113 Tim Bishop
The Thatchers wave goodbye to the Gorbachevs at Heathrow. April 1989
© *The Times*

II4 Chris Harris
Russian leader Mikhail Gorbachev addressing journalists outside
No. 10 Downing Street. April 1989
© *The Times*

115 Bill Cross
Budget day: The Chancellor's wife, Thérèse Lawson. March 1989
© Daily Mail

116   David Rose
Michael Jackson at Wembley Stadium. July 1988
© *The Independent*

117 Nick Rogers
Conservation: Catchers on the Wye. Bailiffs set out as dusk falls to
ambush salmon poachers.
© *The Times*

118 Frank Martin
Preservation: Greenpeace on dolphin watch in Cardigan Bay, Wales. March 1989
© *The Guardian*

120 Bryn Colton
The restored 1920s fishing boat
Excelsior, pictured leaving Lowestoft,
Suffolk.
© *Bryn Colton*

119   David Rose
Wildfowler and dog on the Norfolk Broads.
© *The Independent*

121   Nick Rogers
Brendan Sellick propels his mudhorse across the mud-flats at Bridgwater Bay, Somerset,
near the Hinkley Point nuclear power station, continuing a family tradition
going back at least three generations. Only two families retain the skill to guide the
primitive sledge more than a mile across the mud at low tide to their shrimp nets.
© *The Times*

122   Roger Bamber
Grange-over-Sands quicksand checker.
© *Roger Bamber*

123 Denzil McNeelance
A prostrate protester on Westminster Bridge. The student protest over
the Government's proposed loans scheme ended in the worst student-police
clashes for many years.
© *The Times*

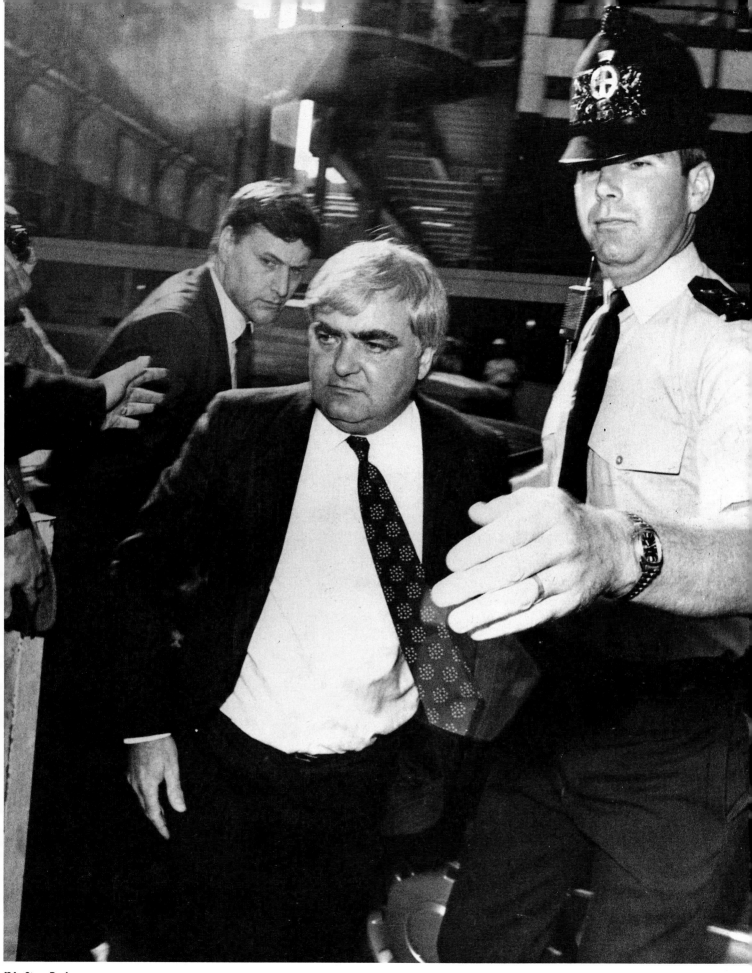

124 Steve Poole
Clowes arrested: Financier Barlow Clowes arrives at Holborn police station, London.
© Daily Mail

125 David Rose
Enjoying a British summer…:
Caister-on-Sea, Norfolk.
September 1988
© *The Independent*

127 Herbie Knott
A wet night in Brighton. May 1988
© *Herbie Knott*

128 David Sillitoe
Press conference for Frank Bruno before his world heavyweight
contest with Mike Tyson.
© *The Guardian*

129 130 Dod Miller
Contestants preparing for the semi-finals of the first Miss USSR competition in a hotel on the outskirts of Moscow. April 1989
© Dod Miller

131 Simon Townsley
Laura, a child at Great Ormond Street Hospital for Sick Children, London.
© *The Sunday Times*

Index
To The Plates

The British Press Photographers' Association Membership

Press photographers lead hectic lives. Chasing news wherever it's happening means being away on assignment most of the time and frequently being out of the country for long stretches. Relying on chance meetings, we quickly lose touch with each other, and this was partly why a group met in 1984 to discuss the idea of an association through which we could bring the best of our photography to a wider audience and give it a longer life than newspapers allow.

The British Press Photographers' Association, which resulted from that discussion, represents and promotes the highest levels of photography within the profession, encourages the best standards of conduct and professional integrity, and works to improve editorial use of photography.

Each year the BPPA presents a major London exhibition and publishes a selection of photographs in book form – both under the title of Assignments, and both collecting members' work from the previous year. Some of the best press photographs fail to get published, and the book and the exhibition thus give us an opportunity to show again, but in more permanent form and under better conditions, not only work already seen but also work that did not – for one reason or another – make it on to the newspaper page.

British photojournalism has never been stronger and never been better appreciated. We are especially lucky to have this year's book – a year when photography's 150th anniversary is being celebrated – edited by our President, Tom Hopkinson, whose work as founding editor of Picture Post made our work possible.

Sir Tom Hopkinson. *Honorary President*
Sue Adler. *The Observer*
Marc Aspland. *Freelance/The Times*
Roger Bamber. *Freelance*
Tim Bishop. *Freelance/The Times*
Jonathon Buckmaster. *Freelance/ Daily Express*
John Chapman. *Freelance*
Stuart Clarke. *Freelance*
Bob Collier. *Sunday Times*
Bryn Colton. *Freelance*
Jez Coulson. *Freelance*
Bill Cross. *Daily Mail*
Stephen Daniels. *Freelance*
John Downing. *Daily Express*
Brian Harris. *Independent*
Chris Harris. *The Times*
Julian Herbert. *Freelance*
David Hogan. *Freelance*
Mike Hollist. *Daily Mail*
Bob Gannon. *Freelance*
Simon Grossett. *Freelance/ Daily Telegraph*
Jon Jones. *Freelance/Independent*
Suresh Karadia. *Freelance*
Martin Keane. *Press Association*
Herbie Knott. *Freelance*
Tony Larkin. *Freelance*
Hilaria McCarthy. *Daily Express*

Denzil McNeelance. *Freelance/ The Times*
Frank Martin. *The Guardian*
Dod Miller. *Freelance*
Dario Mitidieri. *Freelance*
Brendon Monks. *Daily Mirror*
Stuart Nicol. *Freelance*
Ian Parry. *Freelance*
Michael Pattinson. *Freelance*
Mark Pepper. *Freelance/The Times*
Tom Pilston. *Freelance/Independent*
Steve Poole. *Freelance/Daily Mail*
Crispin Rodwell. *Freelance*
Nick Rogers. *Freelance/The Times*
David Rose. *Independent*
David Sillitoe. *Freelance/The Guardian*
Sean Smith. *Freelance/The Guardian*
Michael Steele. *Independent*
Tom Stoddart. *Freelance*
Allan Titmuss. *Freelance*
Simon Townsley. *Sunday Times*
Graham Turner. *Freelance/The Guardian*
Howard Walker. *Sunday Mirror*
Michael Ward. *Sunday Times*
Gareth Watkins. *Reuters*
Alan Weller. *Freelance/The Times*
Geoffrey White. *Life member*
Graham Wood. *The Times*